MOONS

KATE RIGGS

Creative Education • Creative Paperbacks

Published by Creative Education and Creative Paperbacks
P.O. Box 227, Mankato, Minnesota 56002
Creative Education and Creative Paperbacks are imprints of
The Creative Company
www.thecreativecompany.us

Design and production by Chelsey Luther
Printed in the United States of America

Photographs by Corbis (Jon Hicks, Steven Hobbs/Stocktrek Images, Mehau Kulyk/Science
Photo Library, MARK GARLICK WORDS & PICTURES LTD/Science Photo Library, Detlev
van Ravenswaay/Science Photo Library), Defense Video & Imagery Distribution System
(DVIDS), deviantART (AlmightyHighElf), Dreamstime (Oriontrail), Getty Images (SCIEPRO,
Stocktrek Images, Richard Wahlstrom), NASA (NASA/ESA/Hubble SM4 ERO Team, NASA/
JPL/University of Arizona, NASA/JPL-Caltech/STScI, NASA/JPL-Caltech/University of
Arizona, NASA Planetary Photojournal), Shutterstock (leonello calvetti, Elenarts, Tristan3D),
SuperStock (dieKleinert, Robert Harding Picture Library), Wikipedia (Vzb83/NASA)

Library of Congress Cataloging-in-Publication Data
Riggs, Kate.
Moons / Kate Riggs.
p. cm. — (Across the universe)
Summary: A young scientist's guide to natural satellites called moons, including how
they interact with other elements in the universe and emphasizing how questions and
observations can lead to discovery.
Includes bibliographical references and index.
ISBN 978-1-60818-483-5 (hardcover)
ISBN 978-1-62832-083-1 (pbk)
1. Satellites—Juvenile literature. 2. Solar system—Juvenile literature. I. Title.
QB401.5.R54 2015
523.9'8—dc23   2014002416

CCSS: RI.1.1, 2, 3, 4, 5, 6, 7; RI.2.1, 2, 3, 5, 6, 7, 10;
RI.3.1, 3, 5, 7, 8; RF.2.3, 4; RF.3.3

First Edition
9 8 7 6 5 4 3 2 1

Pages 20–21 "Astronomy at Home"
activity instructions adapted from
the Center for Science Education
at UC Berkeley:
http://www.eyeonthesky.org
/lessonplans/12sun_littlemoon.html

TABLE OF CONTENTS

Did you know that moons are called satellites? A satellite orbits, or goes around, something in space. Scientists called astronomers study moons. Earth has one moon. But other **planets** in the **solar system** have more than one.

Two of Saturn's 53 moons

There are 140 satellites, or moons, in the solar system.

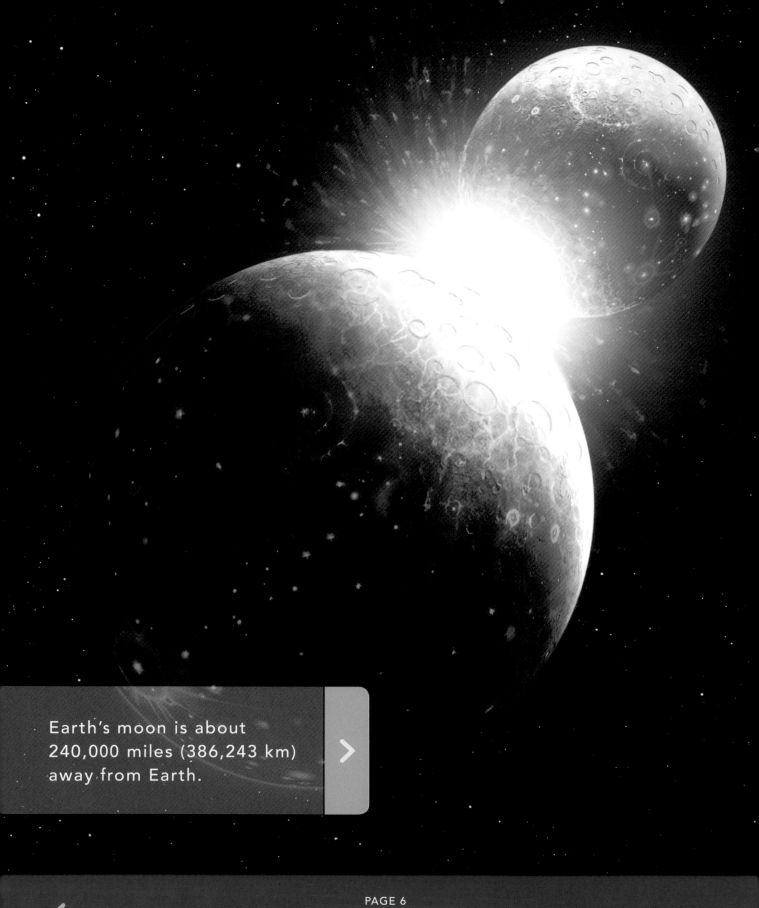

Earth's moon is about
240,000 miles (386,243 km)
away from Earth.

>

←

A long time ago, something the size of Mars ran into Earth. The pieces from that crash probably formed the moon. The moon is rocky. Its top layer is very dusty. **Asteroids**, **meteoroids**, and **comets** hit the moon. They leave holes called craters.

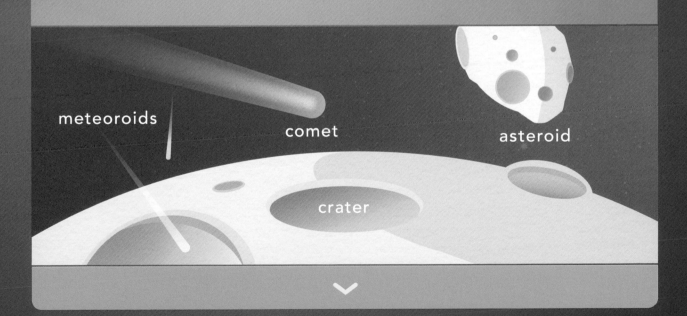

meteoroids

comet

asteroid

crater

The moon does not have air around it. It does not make its own light, either. The sun shines on the moon. What we call "moonlight" is that light from the sun. It takes about 29 days for the moon to go around Earth once.

People used to think that Earth's moon was the only moon in the solar system.

Explorers called astronauts have been to the moon many times since 1969.

Italian astronomer Galileo Galilei found Jupiter's four big moons in 1610.

Most moons around other planets are named for characters from **mythology**. Jupiter has more than 60 moons. The biggest ones are named Io, Europa, Ganymede, and Callisto. Io has active volcanoes! Many moons are just made of ice and rock.

Io

Europa

Ganymede

Callisto

In Greek mythology, Phobos and Deimos were the sons of Ares (the Greek name for Mars).

>

Phobos

Deimos

Mars has two moons. Phobos goes around the planet three times a day. It takes Deimos 30 hours to make 1 orbit. Both moons look lumpy. They have many craters, like Earth's moon.

24 hours

Deimos

Phobos

Mars

"High tide" and "low tide" happen twice a day in all of Earth's oceans.

>

On Earth, ocean tides are controlled by the moon. The moon's gravity pulls on the oceans facing the moon. Oceans on the other side of the planet pull away from the moon. The tides change as Earth spins around the sun.

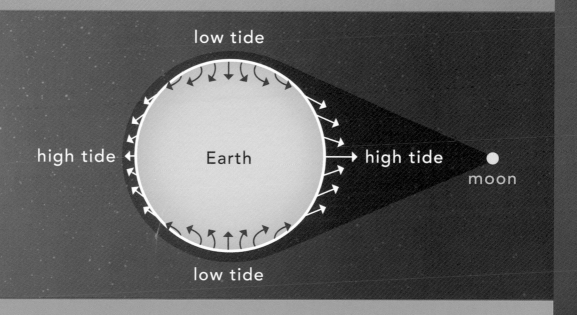

low tide

high tide

Earth

high tide

moon

low tide

Tell someone what you know about moons! What else can you discover?

EARTH

Moon

MARS

Phobos

Deimos

URANUS

Oberon

Titania

JUPITER

Europa

Io

Callisto

Ganymede

SATURN

Rhea

Titan

NEPTUNE

Triton

THE LITTLE MOON HIDES THE SUN

What you need

One small ball and one larger ball

What you do

Set the two balls next to each other on the edge of a table. Kneel down and look at the balls with one eye closed. Move the larger ball (the sun) toward the middle of the table until the two balls look the same size.

What happens if you move the small ball (the moon) in front of the larger one (as shown above)?

	asteroids	big rocks in outer space
	comets	balls of dust and ice from outer space
	meteoroids	chunks of stone or metal traveling through space
	mythology	stories that tell how something came to be
	planets	rounded objects that move around a star
	solar system	the sun, the planets, and their moons

READ MORE

Adamson, Thomas K. *Do You Really Want to Visit the Moon?* North Mankato, Minn.: Amicus, 2014.

Sexton, Colleen. *The Moon.* Minneapolis: Bellwether Media, 2010.

WEBSITES

Astronomy Games for Kids
http://www.kidsastronomy.com/fun/index.htm
Play games to learn more about moons and astronomy.

Quiz Your Noodle: The Moon
http://kids.nationalgeographic.com/kids/games /puzzlesquizzes/quizyournoodle-the-moon/
Test what you know about Earth's moon!

Note: Every effort has been made to ensure that the websites listed above are suitable for children, that they have educational value, and that they contain no inappropriate material. However, because of the nature of the Internet, it is impossible to guarantee that these sites will remain active indefinitely or that their contents will not be altered.

INDEX